# The Poet's Poison

Justine Scott-Gray

# The Poet's Prison

FUZZY FLAMINGO

First published in 2024 by Fuzzy Flamingo
Copyright © Justine Scott-Gray 2024

Justine Scott-Gray: www.drumconsulting.co.uk

Justine Scott-Gray has asserted her right to be identified as the author of this
Work in accordance with the Copyright, Designs and Patents Act 1988.

ISBN: 978-1-7393669-8-8

Illustrations by Morgan Anderson
https://www.instagram.com/pet_semetery

Editing and design by Fuzzy Flamingo
www.fuzzyflamingo.co.uk

A catalogue for this book is available from the British Library.

*To my mum,*
*she had so much love and kindness in her soul*
*but lived with her own secret monster*
*who tormented her to the end*

# Contents

# Introduction

Born in Tavistock in Devon, England, into a naval family with four children, an identical twin, Justine was the quiet one that was just a little different. Born weighing only 2lbs, half the size of her twin sister, Justine was not given the best of starts in life. This may have had a much deeper effect than anyone, including her, ever thought. As her twin was outgoing and demanding, Justine was often encouraged to step back, to give in to her sister, as it was 'easier'.

She often felt different from her siblings, especially her twin, which only increased when they moved to Scotland. As her siblings quickly settled into their new environment, Justine found the gap between them increased to the point when she would find communicating with them difficult. School was tough as she was an undiagnosed dyslexic; she found the environment confusing and became increasingly withdrawn. Justine quickly realised that writing gave her a her way to explore her feelings and bring light to her darkness. In primary school, Justine won a writing competition at only eight years old. Even then, her empathy for the darkness in life was evident as she wrote about a giant who was imprisoned in a dark forest who found friendship in a little girl.

Although her writing gave her great joy, Justine soon realised that she was lagging behind her peers and found reading and spelling a huge struggle. Embarrassed by her poor handwriting and spelling, she stopped writing.

School continued to be difficult; she was often put in the bottom classes where the bullies were, which led to many occasions when she was mentally and physically bullied. One day, while out walking, Justine found some horses in a field. This was something that would change her life forever; they would give her an outlet for her feelings and provide companionship she couldn't find anywhere else. She spent her days watching them, whispering her deep thoughts to them and eventually riding them bareback with string round their necks; she finally felt that she belonged.

Fast forward to her adult life, horses were her constant companion, often owning five or six horses at a time. As time went by, Justine married but never felt truly connected to her husband. She was gifted three children through life and adopted a further boy; these children were her shining lights, keeping her grounded and happy.

There was only one thing that wouldn't shift, that feeling of not truly fitting in, never being completely sure where she belonged; even the horses were starting to lose their calming effect. Then her world changed. Justine's mother was diagnosed with cancer. Although she fought hard, there was no cure, she died peacefully at home. From that point on, life started becoming undone. Justine started numbing this feeling, firstly with work, then family, then alcohol – a glass of wine each night to help the feeling go was the start, but soon it was two or three. But as time went by and the children grew older, the loneliness became overwhelming, dark feelings started growing and soon became an everyday monster to run from. After a number of accidents, she was left in significant pain, walked with a stick and took painkillers each day.

Rock bottom came in December 2018, when her marriage ended. Justine found herself truly alone, her only companion the monster who waited each night to whisper dark words to her. That continued until the 1st of January 2020 when finally the solution came to her, she began to rebuild herself, stopped drinking, started daily exercise and started to read books on psychology and well-being, threw away her walking stick, painkillers and climbed Kilimanjaro. She became a life coach and launched a successful international business. She also began writing poems again. The feelings she had been numbing all her adult life started coming out as poems, writing endlessly each night. She wrote about the darkness in her soul, her fears and her journey of self-discovery and wellness.

This is a collection of poems straight from Justine's heart, her deepest fears, her darkness from her heart and the light that came from taking a healing breath.

# Day One

Day one, it's time, sobriety here I come
I can no longer hide from the pain, remain numb
This is the day
the right day to walk away

Walk away from the disarray
Start to grow not just decay
I deserve more in life
more hope, more care, less strife

Begin the hero's journey, mindset to alter
be my own knight in shining armour
Life is an adventure with dreams and joy
Not a dark prison, a dangerous decoy

So day one here I sit
with so much more to gain than I care to admit
Today I chose to realise my potential
Stop living a life accidental
To live life with real vigour,
Time to fly, become so much bigger

# The Wine Witch

Go on now, it has been a long day
no one will know, care or say
"I'm a better person now, happier, calmer, free"
That sweet, deep warmth you crave is here in this bottle
"It doesn't help me, it dulls my senses, makes me feel useless"

The pain that cripples you will be gone, you'll feel chilled
"The days will be wasted, waiting for that wanting to be fulfilled"
You can keep me secret, no one needs to know
"Everyone always knows, you're no discreet friend"

Without me you are quiet, small, scared
"With you I am loud, crass, ensnared"
But you are too sad, your tears and fears are so bad
"The worries in my head just get worse, I will go mad"

The world doesn't care if you drink
"But I do, I want to fly, grow, not shrink"
You'll never do it, you'll fail
"Let's see my friend, perhaps this time I will prevail"
You'll never do it. You'll fail
"Let's see my friend, perhaps this time I will prevail"

# Fresh Starts

Shining as bright as the brightest day
Light so bright it scares the darkest cloud away
Soul laid bare for my heart to see
Past mistakes healed from the deepest part of me

Warmth now melts my cold façade
Letting in the love I've yearned for in my heart
Gentle thoughts float across my mind
Healed from the pain that left me scarred
living each day without my rusting barbed guard

So how did this transformation take place I hear you ask
How did you quieten your beast within, remove his mask
This was a slow process, but a skill we all possess
Give up the wine that's had you so depressed

Show up to the fight, pick your own battlefield
This time you're the hero, your power no longer concealed
The light that hides has the strength to heal your broken parts
It will illuminate your path with endless fresh starts

# Breaking the Chain

Day draws to dark, the fear rises
Tears in the night, please no more bruises
A day used, a day without praises
No reprises, no one to see the abuses

Escaped, my life to dance at last
Alone but fear remains, pictures of the past
Evenings bring only pain, my private shame
Mind racing, pacing, only myself to blame

My saviour, amber nectar, I'm sold
My evenings are changed, no longer cold
Each day tough but my friend warms my mind
I've finally forgotten my past, left the pain behind

A husband to cherish me, hold me above
A family to care for, children to love
Slowly darkness creeps in, the monster returns
Fire red eyes leave much more than burns

A little girl feels the fear her mum cannot hide
She watches, learns about the monster inside
The monster turns, he sees her there
Nowhere to hide, no one to care
The fear drawn to her, it will take her too
It will invade her thoughts, her invisible tattoo

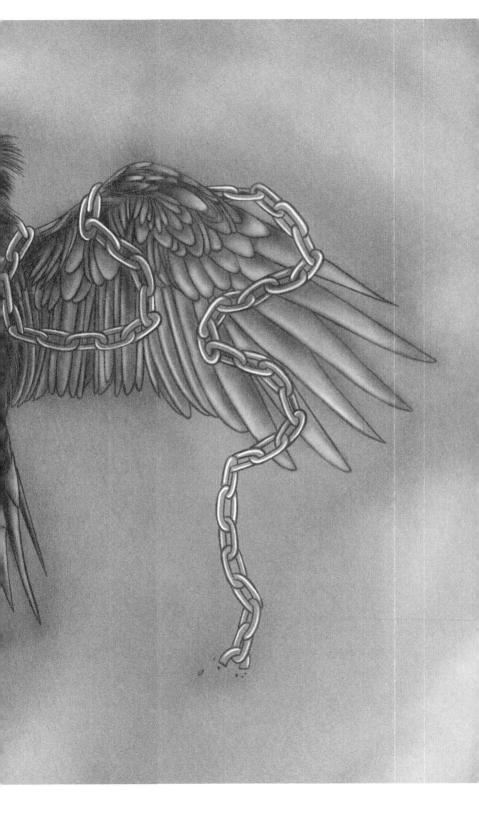

Each night fills her with dark thoughts and anxiety
Fear building, spreading, a time to be wary
Use Mum's solution to scare the monster
She realises too late she is lost, he is her author

Mum is long gone, leaving her monster
Ancient history, the grave of an abuser
Each night the monster grows, nowhere to flee
A chain of fear no one can see
A wounded future she could not foresee

Time to change the script
Can't let her own daughter watch her slip
No, instead she will watch her deny its grip
Today we break the chain, the monster slain
There will be no more pain
The past will not repeat again

# Day One, Again...

Sailing along believing I was fine
I would just say, thanks but I don't drink wine
I felt strong and determined, didn't even notice the decline
Thought the grip of the vine was loosened
That the wine witch had gone, imprisoned

But here I sit feeling like a fool
All those fights won now lost, how insanely cruel
So day one we meet again, not for the first time I choose to
    abstain
This time I pray we will not meet again

# Moonbeams and Mornings

Mind full of lines long drawn;
History of me, the fun's gone
Time to sit down a while
Hear about a new lifestyle

Life without limits, racing wild chariots
Gallop free, time to choose new habits
My body still to my ascension
Raising me to a new dimension

Lifted up among moonbeams
Time to live, realise my dreams
Sore high, fly straight, meditate
Feel the glee, the joy, celebrate

Feelings remembered, an old freedom
Song of memories, a lost asylum
Inside Pandora's box but ready to fall
Beliefs that limit, now hear my call

Noise of a thousand thoughts in me
Falling away, my autumn leaves escaping their tree
Soft and quiet like the embrace of an old friend
Dancing amongst the clouds, I transcend

My mind, at peace, still at last
Silent not sad, I am not my past
Today I chose life, no longer praying for early exits
I deserve the joy, life's merits

# Hidden Words

There she stood, head down, avoiding my stare
She was young, should have been without a care
She had the biggest heart, the kindest way
I knew, she guessed that, eyes that betray

The words burned in my mouth, they felt like fire
Don't say it, don't upset her, be the liar
Make them go away, let them expire

My ears burned as I heard them out loud
Her eyes dart to me, my head in shame bowed
No anger in her eyes, only tears, she doesn't hate me for
    being so bold
She comes to me enveloping me in her soft, loving hold

"I'm so sorry," she mutters, my fears, like snowflakes melt in
    her warm embrace
That day, I said what everyone else wanted to say
I was brave, I thought it would help
Never again would I hear her in pain, never again would I
    hear her sob

He would leave her alone now the booze was gone
Never again would I hide in fear, terrified, alone
But that wasn't it, was it, she didn't quit
She never did

# A New Year – A New Me

Who will I become in 2021?
Will I be a hero, will I become undone?
Will I stay positive, or will I fall?
I have learnt it is up to me, it's my call

I can be the person I want to be
I just need to open my heart and see
2020 has shown me that life is not set
Free flowing and most of all not written yet

2020 showed me I can write, draw, sing and run
It reminded me life is supposed to be fun
I worked, tended my garden
My veg was a source of great adoration
I watched as the world woke up to a new normal
Working from home was okay, we could become less formal

I Zoomed, Skyped but most of all I laughed
I allowed myself to be a little more daft
In 2021 I will be who I want to be, not a victim to circumstance
I will take a chance, I will dance and, most of all, my life I will
    enhance!

# Spring's Sweet Song

Finally, winter has fallen its last flake
Snowdrops line the ground like a frosted lake
My slumber is over, I'm released, awake
Time to begin again, my best life to make

Scent of spring blooms fills my room
Birds dance and sing, released from winter's tomb
Song's perfectly carved angelic anthems
Signalling their joy as warmth becomes

Flowers throw their happiness into the air
Filling the skies with love and care
Sleepy world awakes, smiling over us
Pushing forward, time for our song, our chorus

# Live Your Best Life

The world can be, as they say
anything you like, have it your way
You can choose the fun side of the island
Live in a world permanently brightened
I choose to believe in the positive
Rather than the darker alternative

The treasure in the cave is worth more than diamonds
The darkness holds the confidence to remove your demons
Helps you find the giant that hides within
A wonderful world, ready to begin

You can choose to remove the booze
I promise you; you can't lose
Choose to awake the giant
no longer a prisoner to the wine on which you were once
    reliant!

# The Mountain

Tears from angels dampen my face
Up here in the hills, my dark happy place
I feel her breath under my boots
Silently my soul finds deeper roots

Black silence rings in my ears
Her savage river flowing over my fears
Air scented sweet with earthy decay
My mind free to wander, content to stray

Alone but not lonely, engulfed in wilderness
Quietly with her, I count my blessings
Love inside me glows, my internal sunlight
Solitude, my fuel, set to ignite
Life is not for merely surviving
It is for burning bright, clinging to rocks and climbing

Up in the clouds where heaven sits
Wild beauty within the summits
But she will not give her freedom away

# Blackbird Song

Blackbird revealing your sad, lonely song
Cutting me open with beautiful birdsong
Notes piercing the morning air so sweet, so strong
Day has started, full of fear headlong

Misery likes company and so you have me
High up in the tree for all to see
Wish I could sing my tears to the world
Deepest sadness that engulfs me never to be told

Black as my darkest thoughts, your feathers shine
Eyes glow like burning candles of a shrine
Private pain hiding behind bottles of wine
Each morning you sing my pain to me
Each morning recording my steady decline

# An Extra 6"

An extra 6" for my heels please
Just wood, no fuss no glitz
A box made for me I'll never see
My heart will be quiet by then
A silent, peaceful end, amen

Don't think I'm gone, I'm not in that box
I'm in the clouds, on the hills, melted into rocks
The love in my heart now soaring high, burning bright
Your own beautiful moonlight

Death feels so quiet, so final
A life of sorts, accidental, gone now
My life slipped out the door
Nothing left to explore
6" for my heels, today I want to look taller than before

# Just One...

They say, go ahead, just have one, it won't hurt but it does
It hurts deeply, it burns, it scalds
It holds, it hides you away, it makes you choose
In the end, there is only one truth, you will lose

# Blackbird Sobriety Song

Blackbird singing your seductive song, love on fire
Telling the world that spring is here, full of desire
Lying here listening I realise what I missed
Choked on life, in bed with my personal agonist

New day giving birth to a new me
Tears dried, showing up for all to see
Full of kindness, no longer sad and hollow
The time has come to live, fly like a swallow

Each morning your song reminds me
Tomorrow is not promised, cannot be borrowed
Each morning your secret song is just for me
I smile knowing I'm no longer a detainee

The song that once signalled pain
Wakes me to start my amazing journey again
Each note perfectly carved dances in the air
Natural ebb and flow of hopes you share

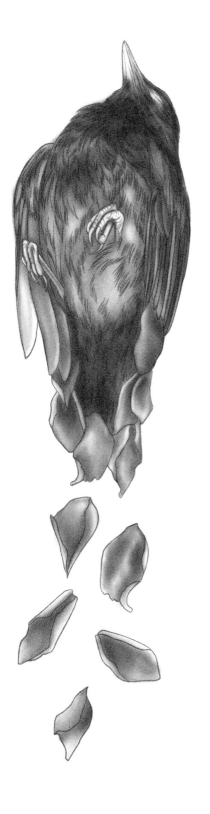

# The Fighter

Dear girl what are you waiting for?
Lying there cold on the floor
Get up, you don't belong there
It's time to open your wings and soar

Those tears won't make the pain go away
The monsters will only stay
Feel the dead air in your lungs leave
Breathe in the angels' gaze, believe

You were born to fly, fight, win
Slay those dark thoughts within
Starlight in your eyes
Clouds of moon dust from your cries
You are enough, she made you tough

# The Warrior

Mountaintop where the clouds lift
See your true path, your gift
She will keep your secrets safe, whisper into her dark earth
Feel the wind lifting you higher
Skywards to her heart's savage fire

The mountain, with her deep roots in the world
Hot lava veins entwined, curled in savage defiance
She does not fear the darkness or the monsters
She was made of greater things, she won't kneel at any altars

Above the land of the living where few dare to tread
She lies in majestic glory with her secrets unsaid

# The Robin

Good morning said the little robin, why are you here all alone?
I'm waiting said the woman with sadness in her eyes
Why are you waiting for something on that cold, old stone?
For my life to restart, for the joy I no longer see
Waiting for the love and laughter to again be

But why wait here, so cold in the darkness?
This is where they left me with faces full of sadness
Waiting for them to come back to me, remove this emptiness

The robin knew why the lady was there full of regret
He saw what she could not yet
The life wasted, her steady decline
The wine she'd tasted, her own shrine

He saw her choose to drink away her days
A family begging her to change her ways
Now here she was in the place where it ends
The place where the soul transcends

She didn't know it yet but it was all too late
No more tomorrows, no more love, no more hate
The robin watched as the lady waited that day
He watched, he didn't tell her, he didn't say
As night fell the darkness came and took her away

# Mum

This is how I remember you
Eyes hazelnut brown, sparkling like morning dew
A smile so soft and knowing
Skin like sunrise, vibrant and glowing

Your smell was like a warm embrace
It engulfed me, my happy place
Like music playing far away, you drifted off slowly
You tried but you couldn't stay

You were my protector, my mum
Never thought one day you'd be gone
Waves of pain washing over me, leaving me for dead
Cancer that couldn't be healed is what they said

But you are still here, your eyes welcoming
My shining light, my inspiration
Every time I look in the mirror you are there
Every inch of me you made with loving care
The mountain, the girl, together they keep the darkness at bay

# Do Not Cross the Tracks

Heart thumping, train beckons
Time to kill these private assassins
Rattling, screaming, mind broken
Silence the cries, a death unspoken

It's here, no more time
Yeah, I know it's a terrible crime
Noisy children play on board
Commuters poking keyboards
Writing emails on the lines
Absently going out of their minds

Gone, my mind, my pain, my life
Brakes scream in anger and disbelief
Fatality on the track, scarlet-soaked rails
Quiet, dark, no more fails
Dead, a silent heart
The end, my soul torn apart

# In the Garden of My Mind

My garden has many flowers
bright, beautiful and fun
The trees grow straight as if reaching for the sun
The birdsong echoes a life without care
The scent of a million petals lies calmly in the air

But under the flowers lies a darker place
Where hurt and pain lie in wait
Where the sadness and regret come to die
Where the seeds must fight to see the sky

Death, yes it lives here too
Tucked up in all that's growing and new
To be born is also to die
This is where we say our final goodbye

But the dark place is where the growing begins
It's not in the flower or the bird that sings
In the darkest place lies the greatest treasure
Our new beginning, the starting point from where we measure

Don't choose to smell only the roses
Feel the pain as it decomposes
For we are under there, waiting to be free
A small acorn turning into the tallest tree

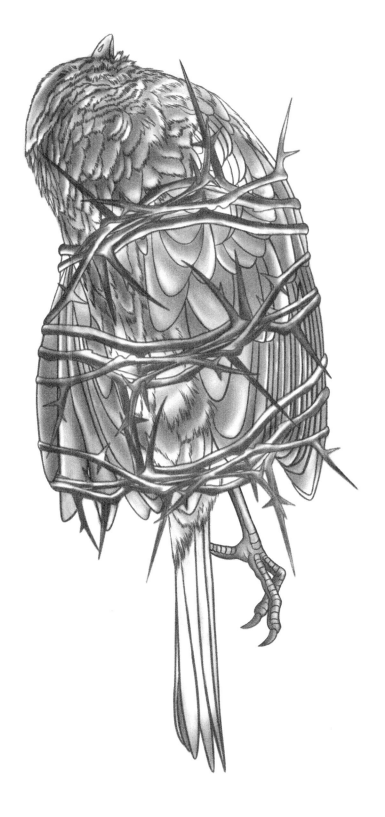

# I Made a Boy

I made a boy with the biggest heart
But watched as the world tore it apart
I made a boy, grew him all on my own
His dad had left us all alone

I made a boy with the kindest way
Cried when they wanted to take him away
I made a boy with love in his eyes
No one to hear us, our silent cries

I made a boy who loves me so
Holding me tight, he lets his love flow
I made a boy with laughter in his voice
I watch him show the world there is always a choice

# Seduction in Suspension

Flowing notes dance in knowing hands
His muse lifts as each note lands
Her body still to her ascension
Raising her high, a new dimension

Rhythmically, magically floating upwards
The dark piano plays its melodies skywards
Eyes burning, so dark, so still
Strokes from notes stealing her will

Hypnotised, a seduction so sweet
Her heart soothed, quietly it submits
Elevated for all to see, a dance of ebb and flow
Songs of a thousand violins lock them in their private show

# A Place to Hide

Stay small said the voice, stay quiet as a mouse
Your fractured mind needs time to heal
your broken heart, not theirs to steal
In a place of stilted solitude
you practise your thankless gratitude

The darkness keeps your secrets safe
Kept clear of life's burning chafe
Show no one your hiding place
Your guilt, your hurt, your private disgrace

Stay quiet, they won't know your pain
Keep to the shadows, safe inside your tortured brain
One day your strength will return
You will feel bold, strong, truly reborn

For now, enjoy the trees, the birds, the earth
Wallow in the dark peaty recesses until your rebirth
Your new life awaits you like a spring morning
Fresh, sparkling, adorning you with happiness soaring

# The Quiet Ones

Watch the quiet ones, the ones with sadness in their veins
Hearts heavy with dark musings
Lungs filled with damaged air
No longer able to count their blessings

They keep to the shadows,
Simply waiting to decompose
They won't be too much, loud
They'll stay hidden in the crowd.
Slipping away on their private curse
Watch the quiet ones, they are always worse

# Blue Dress

Twin dresses for twin girls
Party dresses, swirls and twirls
Hand stitched by old hands
Time taken with care and love
Perfect make, fit like a glove

Twin dresses in red and blue
Blue, so cold, so mute
Colours to match, colours to suit
A sister, so bubbly, so cute

Identical dresses for biological blessings
My beginnings with difficult feelings
One so loud, elevated
Other quiet, tolerated

Why couldn't both be red, why blue instead?
Just a small girl, a scared kid
Outside, cold running through thin skin
Hardly noticed Mother taking the portrait

Wearing granny's dress of blue
This twin's dress has a different hue
Little flowers, ribbon round waist
A memory, a feeling retraced

Old hands cold now, long gone
Dresses long lost, lines long drawn
Twin moments over the years
Same feelings linger, eyes filled with tears
An ageing mind remembers young fears

# You Left

One day I woke up without you
My love, you left without a word
The warmth that you gave has gone cold
Whisperings of love left untold

I didn't see it coming, see the warning
Never felt you leave that desperate morning
In that space in between awake and slumber
My love left, slipped into a new adventure

Now I sleep with a silent heart
No words can ease my pain, no healing can start
On the floor lies the shattered pieces of my mind
No love to warm my soul, no happiness to find

# Standing on Gravestones

Dyslexic, disorganised, disaster
Don't teach, she can't learn, she doesn't matter
Sitting in the back, she'll never impress
Just look at her work, untidy, a mess

Just another child we can't teach
Another doley in the making, the system's leech
This one has no ability, she won't shine
She'll find her way on the production line

After a while she won't question why
She'll just lie low, won't even try
There is no choice with these ones
The children the system abandoned

Abortions of the institutions
No budget, no time, no solutions
Hush child, no one cares
Sit in those chairs at the back, hide your despairs

A future, I suppose you do
But not successful, best restrict your view
Kids like you don't fly high
Be happy with your lot, just comply

# The Darkness

I feel it coming, hardly there like the ghost of a fire
Embers of sadness laced with dark attire
My old companion with its deathly grip
Dragging me down, laughing as I trip

Darkness injected again into my veins
The black, sticky bitterness remains
Drawn to my pain like a moth to a flame
Breathing in my fear, whispering secrets for none to hear

Eyes closed to the joy of living
My mistakes, there's no forgiving
Silence screams at me from the night
My own private battle, my endless fight

Pulling myself free from the dark
I will burn like fire, life's sacred spark
Climb higher where the hurt can't reach you
Cling to the mountain, just hold on, trust the view

Ferns like stallions, sunny manes flowing in the wind
Heather blue and green, beautifully entwined
This is the place where I am defined
Summits of ancient rock that heal
My solid place no one can steal

My mountain, my saviour thank you

# Spring Will Follow

As the days get shorter, the nights colder
Each passing day sees us older
Remember we are but part of life's rich tapestry
We are all saplings in the world's ageing forestry

This is your day, your glorious prize
Trust in nature, the sun will rise
Bathe in her loving, warm glow
The icy north wind will blow
Mountain rivers will always flow

Maybe the rain will turn to snow
Covering babies' faces below
Its time to be steady, to be slow
Don't rush, don't focus on the woe
If winter comes, spring will surely follow

# Candlelight

Flickering, dancing afterglow
Life illuminated in a window
A window into a soul long lost
A soul that's spent all its cost

The distant beat of a drum
The sound quietens, the time has come
Breath stilted, faintly there
Lungs choking on once sweet air

Light leaves her eyes, she sleeps
A sleep without end, it's time to descend
Warm hands grow cold, lips blue
No more life, no more you

The earth keeps moving, spinning, ageing
My world has stalled like a broken engine
No reason, no sense, no why
Why today my mum had to die

# Adrift

Darkness, the soft blanket of darkness
Soft, sticky, sweet, hiding my shame
No light, I need the dark, but light came
The pain, shards of memory pierce my head
Cutting, wounding, leaving me for dead

Who did I talk to, kiss, hug, pester?
Where is my phone, purse, my heart beats faster
I'm so embarrassed, last night was a disaster
Wine is not my saviour; it is my cancer
Never again, I must find a new answer.

# Gift

Sun rising, awake, shining, smiling
A gift, a treasure, a day compiling
Clear head, no sickness, no reconciling
Last night's revelling, me behaving
There was no endless craving

Dance? Not me, not sober!
But I chatted, laughed, I was fully present
Friends abundant, I was not absent
I was the enthusiast; I am not my past

# Angels without Wings

So here I sit, my broken heart, pieces of a rainbow on the floor
My heart didn't smash in one go, it took years until I couldn't
cope anymore
I drank to numb the pain, I told myself that I would be okay
Distracted myself with noise and chaos, but couldn't ever
truly get away
So I decided it was time to call it a day
Time for me to face the pain that was hiding deep inside, stop
the decay

I joined OYNB, met a tribe, they welcomed me in and gave
me hope
Day one, two and three done, finally on the right slippery
slope
Wine witch was dead, what next, who am I, what shall I do?
Self-development here I come, I'm ready to start anew

A new tribe was needed for this task, one that saw the
potential behind the fear
Office athletes with their leader Andy Ramage, a true
pioneer!
I joined them, feeling every bit the broken child I'd left behind
Showed them my broken pieces, my dark mind

They came, like a wave of love and acceptance
Picking up my broken pieces with true diligence
Each live, each like repaired the shards of my broken heart
They listened to my deepest, darkest secrets hidden in my art

The words spilled out of my mind like hot lava
I wrote what I could not say, my own amnesia
I found a home with this tribe of angels without wings
My tribe of friends, true AF kings and queens

They all came, they picked up the shards of my heart
Broken but not lost, just torn apart
They placed them in the void where once they'd sat
They helped me mend my broken thoughts, my negative chat

# Her Time

The final tearstain
No more pain
Nothing else to gain
She won't laugh again

Empty eyes stare into the abyss
Lips holding the ghost of her kiss
Skin no longer glowing, now porcelain
She is gone, I won't hold her again

She can now fly
Gravity gone, silver linings when you die
She is with her cherished ones
She will hold them until our time comes

# A Girl Called Gratitude

That voice that helps me see joy came back today
I didn't ask her where she'd been as I knew she wouldn't say
Whispering to me, time for your darkness to rest
This is your time to fly, feel the love in your chest

Feel your life as the beautiful gift you've been given
Not the cold and dark place, your handmade prison
Nor the curse you try to escape from in the bottom of the
    bottle
Your life was meant to shine, it wasn't accidental

Stop listening to the voices that tell you you're not good
    enough
Leave them to die in the dark, don't pay their tariff
See the amazing life you have and smile; sit with me for a
    while
Be grateful for your gifts, see the soft glow of your smile

# 365 Days AF for Me

I am optimistic today; the future is mine to own
I have a new plan, new skills to hone
The space you gain is amazing
Finally, you have time to do some appraising

The real you is hiding but ready to be reborn
You are in the earth, a foetus, an acorn
You are at the feet of your best life, your new adventure
Ready to become your own champion, a real achiever

With the help of a steady tribe, you start out
First few days are tough but they remove your doubt
They share their highs and their lows
They open their hearts, their love flows

Without them you'd be lost
Stick with it or you may pay the highest cost

# The Phoenix from My Ashes

Smile when I'm gone, for I'll be watching
Laugh when you're sad, there's no sense in wailing
Stand firm when pain comes that day
It won't treat you kindly either way

In dark eyes of pain you'll find strength
Dive into the fire, soak it up
Live a life adorning, no days of mourning
Just turn the sadness into a fuel
Take the pain, use it to help you sparkle

Don't hide, you've dragons to slay
Shine bright, little star, light the way
Be yourself, for you are amazing
Stay the crazy girl I've been raising

# Monsters Don't Live under Duvets, Do They?

Hiding in bed, waiting for my mind to mend
Safe, the warmth embraces me like an old friend
But recently I worry I'm not alone
My normal quiet is noisy, a messy cyclone
But monsters don't live under duvets, or at least it's never
    been known

Softness of pillow turns to sharpness of thorns
Warmth to bitter cold, something forewarns
Recently a darker feeling, one I cannot keep at bay
But monsters don't live under duvets, or so they say

As day draws to a close, my monster awaits
A space just before sleep he hides and waits
I never see him coming, although history dictates I should
But monsters don't live under duvets, although I suppose
    they could

My mind full of ashes from fires long dead
Shadows of moments from words once said
Mind retracing each moment of shame
He's drawn to my pain like a moth to the flame
But monsters don't live under duvets, or maybe they do…

# Perfection Is Heaven

Glistening in the sun above the clouds
Wings outstretched I dive towards the crowds
Faster and faster I go, pushing my limits
I am a gull in a place no gull inhabits
The cold feels like the warm embrace of a friend
The noise of a thousand thoughts fills my head

This place like the corner of my mind that's just for me
Here where I am accepted, where I am free
Plummeting through the air
Thoughts releasing like leaves from a tree
I am a pioneer, there are no judgments here
Air stinging my eyes, pulling my wings
I ascend, feathers flying, my soul sings

I am Jonathan Livingston Seagull, the gull that changed the
    rules
I am unlike the gulls chasing scraps, those poor misguided
    fools
I am flying, diving, spinning and soaring
My life once meaningless and boring
Now full of risks, happiness and exploring

I am my own hero, a shining light
I know the more I push the harder the fight
The higher I go, the harder I fall
But I was not born to follow
I am a gull with a desire to fly
Every day choosing not to die
Choosing each day to find my flow, my glee
A life racing the sun over the land and sea

I wait for them to cheer and praise my efforts
Instead, I'm banished, sent to the outskirts
The shame, my family's name, my pain, my blame
The hurt goes deep, it slices my heart
Their eyes stare, they don't see potential
To them I'm damaged goods, clearly mental

I am alone, the disapproval is everywhere
Isolated, my mind full of sadness and despair
I am supposed to lead, to fly, to succeed
I have to leave this place of regret
Time now to stay my path, time to forget
Days now to be filled with practising skills
Free, no rules, just drills and thrills

Blinded by the light I keep pushing my limits
I will be the gull that the world inherits
A gull, yes, but I will be the best gull I can be
Perfection is heaven, it's not a place you can see
Keep growing, learning, be forevermore a trainee

# The Swan

Eyes dark as oceans deep
Full of secrets for her to keep
Knowing eyes that have felt true pain
Memories of friends she won't see again

Calmly she rests in still reflection
Fear masked by God-given perfection
Danger looms in the darkness, no sleep
Fear her constant companion buried deep

Elegant glides hide frantic kicking
Prey always know murder is beckoning
Silent curves of snow pure wings
Pull her into the sky, safe from hurtful things

She has no need to count her blessings
Her struggles hidden from view, private misgivings
Strong and fierce but always graceful
The swan, the river's perfect white angel

# Death and Her Friends

Death does not ask permission
It does not need submission
It drifts in on a Monday morning with no invitation
Casting a darkness into life, removing all illumination

Death does not come alone, it brings its friends
Fear and tears, until sadness descends
It won't care if they are in their prime
You can't ask for more time

The end of a life accidental
No more laughter, curtain call final
Into the darkness and unknown destination
No more life, a final cessation

Printed in Great Britain
by Amazon